LAK[illegible]OP

Mountain Bike Ride

by Tim Woodcock

First published in book form in 1994 by Future Books

This revised edition published in 1998
by
Mountain Bike Routes UK
45 Lyewater, Crewkerne, Somerset TA18 8BB

If you would like more information on other cycle route guides from
MBRUK please write to:
The Publisher, MBRUK at the address above, e-mail at
info@mbruk.co.uk or via our web site at *www.mbruk.co.uk*

CONTENTS

THE LAKELAND LOOP

THE RIDE

The Lakeland Loop is the most challenging, long-distance off-road ride in England. It's also the most spectacular. So if you're looking for the ride of a life-time, one that's crammed with just about everything that's great about off-roading, take up the challenge.

It describes a tortuous circuit through one of the most popular and beautiful National Parks in the world. Dramatic crags and ridges tower over placid lakes to create a concentrated landscape that is Alpine in grandeur yet intimate in proportion. From the wild, sweeping fells of High Street beset by 1000' cliffs to the bleak, mine-torn moors round the Back 'O Skiddaw and on up through the mountain fastness of Borrowdale, over the deep divide of Wasdale, across the contorted crags of Dunnerdale for a final run through the rugged forests of Grizedale. The Lakeland experience is an intoxicating blend of awesome landscapes and the intimate encounter between terrain and tyre.

THE RIDER

There's no doubt that off-roading in the fells of Cumbria is a unique experience. It's undoubtedly tough but then that's part of the challenge that pitting your wits, fitness and skills against the might of real mountain passes is about. "No pain, no gain" is an oft quoted adage that's particularly apt to off-road cycling. Even more so where mountains are concerned when pain, height-gain and enjoyment follow hard upon the heels of the other. There's precious little in the way of vistas when you're stuck in a valley bottom but up on the giddy heights of High Street a Lakeland tableau sweeps away from under your feet. It's breath- taking and an exhilaration that's well worth the effort.

So we're talking fit. Not only cycling fit but hiking fit too - there's one or two bike-carries plus a push or three. But then I'm no duathlete, have bike skills that would be eclipsed by any sprog worth their salt and most of my riding has been limited to 20 mile day-loops. I tackled each challenge on it's own. Another mountain, another pass, another day. Then suddenly the ride is done and I'm left with a curious mixture of elation, achievement and regret.

THE ROUTE

150 miles of knee-jerk downhills where treads spit grit and hot blocks cream rims grey; white- water fords split in arcs of silver spray; sensuous singletrack - eyes down, bike skipping; shredding the edge of awesome, yawning gaps backed by some prime-time scenic displays of splendid proportions. This route's about riding in the wilds. It's not tied to an attempt to encompass every lake, or mountain or dale. In consequence we encounter the most scenic, the most radical and the most satisfying off-roading that The Lakes have to offer.

Why start from Windermere? The pastoral setting of this, the Lake District's largest stretch of water, gives you a chance to settle into the swing of off-roading before hitting the high fells. Taking it counter-clockwise the Lakeland Loop kicks off with the more rounded, rideable, biker-friendly eastern fells saving the steeper, western slopes for the end when your skills have been finely honed by five days on the hills. It also hits most of the higher peaks and passes - High Street, Honister and Black Sail for instance - from their 'good' side.

Tim Woodcock 1998

SUMMARY:

Meandering circuit of the Lake District National Park with wet-weather, extreme terrain detours. Not for the tyro, nor the less-than-fit. Suits hostelling and supported touring.

TERRAIN:

Mountainous and difficult in places with at least two major carries to negotiate. That aside this route's got a big measure of singletrack - some exceptionally fine riding. Navigation is mostly straightforward in good conditions.

LOOPING THE LOOP

The 'faff' factor was running high. Despite days of careful preparation John (my partner for the tour.) and I found ourselves adjusting brakes (again!), tweaking gears and fixing an overnight puncture. Infuriating! But a bunch of minor 'mechanicals' was a mere glitch in the grand scheme of things.

Our grand scheme was 150 miles of fell-riding, taking in some of the finest off-roading in Europe and the tour would take six days. Day on day of real mountain biking, lured on by pathways new, complete with passes and peaks to conquer, sinuous singletrack to scintillate and twisting trails to test our technical skills to the limits. And beyond. No wonder the anticipation factor was running high and frustration was knocking at the door! But we were free and away; kicking cranks before a shadow was cast.

We (for our first day we were joined by Pete Davies, the National Park's area manager.) wound our way up from Windermere's windy shore. The persistent clack-clack of rigging lapping mastheads faded away, the tarmac hill-climbs dropped behind us and we hit the first track to feel a heart-warming rumble from the tyres.

Spring had sprung, sun flickered through bright new leaves and John was jumping anything on the trail that cast a shadow. Way-out west we caught a glimpse of Walna Scar. A classic mountain pass that we'd be hammering down in a few days time. The prospect was pure pleasure.

In the meantime the grand shoulders of High Street (the name given both to the mountain and the roman road that traverses it.) were thrusting south, building our horizon ahead. To John, a newcomer to the Cumbrian Mountains, the massed summits ahead was an awesome prospect but before he could consider the climb we dipped left for the gritty, knuckle-jarring descent through the chicanes of Garburn Road. Hikers and hackers were wending their way up so we pulled aside for the thirty-odd nags, lads and lasses as they headed for the Pass. A busy road but the trail down into Troutbeck was empty and trouble-free. John put the hammer down, I skipped and skidded in his wake, and we flew down the first few hundred yards of High Street.

It may have been straight as a die in roman times but now it sports some tastefully arranged twists and turns. Strange to think we were making tyre tracks on a road trod by legionaries, marching to a bleak and hostile outpost in an empire that crumbled more than a millennia past.

Just as we were wondering when serious height-gain was to start Park Fell's precipitous slopes loomed ahead. On its flank was etched a series of sinuous switch-backs that climb 700' onto to the saddle of Ill Bell. A quick R 'n R stop by the gate at the bottom then it was framesets on shoulders, heads down, hike and hum a ditty to deter the bike-carry blues. A bit of bog served as a signpost to detour over the top. End of carry, then to turnabout and drink in the vast panorama spread out below. Westward, fellsides stepped down to Windermere; a glittering lakeland limb set in a remote, rolling landscape. No wonder so many wordsmiths have been inspired to wax lyrical about The Lakes.

The day's big climb was bagged. We turned to where two posts stood, like sozzled sentries, at the beginning of an awesome piece of singletrack that clings to the ledge above Gavel Crags. The narrow path wends its way round the lip of a crumbling cliff top. A hang-glider's delight but for us a 1000' flight for any mistakes. I like life and so we walked! The well-worn trail to High Street's summit was peppered with pedestrians so we elected to turn aside from the summit (it's a footpath and we wanted to stay in the saddle.) and follow the bridleway instead. A rocky little path that passes perilously close to a dizzy drop-off with Hayeswater as a distant splash-down.

Definitely shredding the edge with a dash of exhilaration thrown in! We lingered a while in the sun-baked shelter of the wall on the Straits if Riggindale before setting off for the roller-coaster run to Loadpot Hill. The jagged crags of Rampsgill and High Raise gave way to sweeping shoulders of moor interspersed with streaks of sodden peat. Some deep, some not. Flushed with success at steaming through a series of shallow peat pits, John hit a hub- deep hole, enjoyed impromptu air-time and grounded with a grunt. We laughed. All the same we were a cautious trio for a time, then we'd get cocky, turn on the speed and one of us would execute yet another endo.

Down round the shoulder of Loadpot Hill the trail twists and turns through a delightful little gully that invites you to take time-out from gravity. Late afternoon and a dearth of other trail- users gave us an excuse to hammer so, with John hard on my heels, we played close pursuit all the way down to The Cockpit. Bog-grabbers permitting!

The mires round the foot of Barton Fell had the visuals firmly ground-bound. When we looked up the spectacular view across a serpentine stretch of Ullswater backed by the ragged ridge of Helvellyn stopped us in our tracks. Stunning! We should have lingered longer but the next few miles were destined to top off a day of brilliant trail-blazing with a technical edge. I'd ridden it before and was keen to have the others experience it.

Beyond Sandwick the trail narrows to singletrack, things get tricky and I bailed out on a boulder-strewn chicane that Pete coursed through with consummate ease. No harm done but I nearly lost the bike in the lake! Patterdale saw the end of that ribbon of rough delight and the end of a fine day of fell riding.

SKIP AND SKID ROUND SKIDDAW

The heights of Helvellyn were hidden in swathes of swirling vapour, the odd patch of snow still visible in the northern crevasses. Spring obviously hadn't penetrated to those peaks but here below daffodils danced yellow in the breeze, all Wordsworthian and wonderful.

John was paying the penalty for that High Street endo - a sore shoulder and stiff limbs. My extra-bike activities had cost me the odd graze and bruise but nothing serious. The legs were feeling the first day's foray across the fells though! So the road cruise round the perimeter of Ullswater was an ideal leg-stretcher that put us in good stead to tackle the long climb up through Dockray - two miles of tarmac that I'd been dreading. The map contours had over-dramatised the gradient and we clocked into the Old Coach Road track with our off-road appetites well whetted.

Low cloud swirled round the Dodds, formed, reformed and spat sultry spots of rain at us. Out on the bleak, brown fells a sea of mist hugged the tarnished reed beds to create the illusion of a bronzed, ethereal seascape. I was glad we weren't out on a 'bricht, moonlit nicht'!

We hummed along, slicing through puddles, hopping the central ridge, having a good time when we were brought up short by the sight of a 4x4 jeep, set at a jaunty angle and stranded in a mire. Strapped to the back were a pair of rather tasty Kona MTBs. Odd? The owners could've ridden out and had a good off-road blast into the bargain! Must have been posers - judging by the distinctly town-type treads they were toting.

Round the Knotts of Threlkeld the track took a downward turn, we took on speed for a fast'n loose, tail skipping descent where every wayward wheel slide had my heart skip a beat. One mean, adrenaline inducing run - especially the tarmac hump that lurks like a sleeping hippo on the lower slopes. Watch out when you fly through! When we finally spewed out onto the road in the Vale we both had the feeling we'd had a lucky plummet. A touch more twist, an extra grain of gradient and we'd have wiped out with rocks on! Up there brakes were just a temptation from the Devil.

The hushed hum of knobblies on the road melded into the roar of traffic hurtling down the A66. Suddenly life on the 'outside' hit us hard. We played an unwilling game of chicken with thundering juggernauts, took off into Threlkeld and were only too glad to hear the din dim into the distance. Under a skyline dominated by the cliffs and crags of Blencathra - a black name in the world of mountaineering - we climbed round Blease Fell on the old mine road to the long abandoned Glenderaterra workings and into an impressive valleyscape. Then the final haul up to the Cumbria Way had us beat. It was down to bad choice of line - by me, a lack of commitment to conquer the climb and laggardly limbs. John's aching shoulder was giving cause for concern too.

I was now on familiar territory. The Back 'o Skiddaw (pronounced Skidder) route was my initiation into Lakeland mountain biking - many moons ago - and I was keen to get on to the White Water Dash descent. It's every bit as good as it sounds - providing it's clear of hikers. But first we had a gloopy, granny-cog grind up to Skiddaw House YHA. Just the right goo to test tyre traction to the limits. A long, low, grey-clad building Skiddaw House stands alone at the head of the Caldew valley and is one of the few YHAs accessible only to hikers and bikers. No screaming school kids here!

John spied the rough 'n ready track down to the Caldew river, let out a whoop (actually, mountain bikers never do that accept in the videos), hit the cranks and sped off. Obviously we'd been climbing too long! But we still had a climb or two, albeit short ones, before tasting the delights of the Dash downhill.

At last gravity was going our way again, the path was pedestrian-free and I was just raring to go. We spun cranks, hit forty-plus then life concentrated into steering a course through a blurred mass of scattered rocks with a slip-stream roaring in the ears. Suddenly the track twists in a tight bend with enough slip to give the adrenaline factor a kick sky-wards then it's back to earth to open the gate above the Dash Falls. I jumped off, opened the gate expecting to see John hurtle on through. Quiet (bar a bit of heart pummel). No sign of him up the track and, fearing the worst, I climbed back up through the bends. A sorry silhouette appeared on the skyline. John wheeling his bike. A pinch puncture had put paid to his dash to the Dash.

With the flat fixed (we were also in the right spot to take in sweeping views over the Solway to Scotland which I'd missed on the first run.) I got a second crack at those bends - a beautifully placed berm keeping it all on course - and opened the gate to give John a clear run over rock strata steps with a serving of scree and another bend to liven it up. His beatific grin and bright eyes were ample proof that a mere puncture wasn't going to ruin this run. Then the Dash descent was done and we spun out onto the quiet lanes by Bassenthwaite. An ominous scrape-scrape emanating from my rear wheel signalled a mechanical problem. A broken spoke.

Nothing for it but to detour down to Keswick, call in to the Keswick Mountain Bike Centre and take it from there.

Out of all bad comes some good. KMBC's manager, Amos, replaced the spoke, trued the wheel, put John in touch with a local physiotherapist and volunteered as trail companion while John was getting a day's rest and manipulation. Plus an unscheduled overnight at Derwent Water YHA that treated us to a spectacular dawn over the motionless mirror that was the lake. Stunned by such sylvan, sunlit beauty I plum forgot to take on board the day's weather forecast. A mistake I was to pay for later.

DEEP INTO DERWENT

I teamed up with Amos back at KMBC. Together with two other lads we got a lift back to Bassenthwaite to pick up where John and I had left off. The day was bright and balmy with just a whisper of wind so, with John on furlough, I took the opportunity to shed some kit and travel light. Once again we kicked off with a gentle road cruise along shadow-dappled lanes to stretch taught sinews. We generated enough heat on the climb up into the forest above Bassenthwaite Lake to strip off wind-proof tops and cruise. Summer had arrived at last! The downhill dash through Wythop woods with the wind whistling, sunlight flashing and tagging onto Amos's fast disappearing tail dispelled lazy, hazy-day reveries in an instant. Back to track and some summertime trail-shredding with a vengeance!

We quit the forest, breezed through Braithwaite, crossed the Newlands valley and hooked up on the Cat Bells bridleway. A well-graded ribbon of off-roading that roller-coasts its way up into Borrowdale with a silver-speckled Derwent Water spread out below. Down a tightly stepped, wall-hemmed path - walls are pretty magnetic this close - we shot out onto a steep, slippery, roughly paved slope for a final run-out to the road.

During our scenic saunter along the slopes of Cat Bells Nature had been brewing up a storm. Dark clouds scudded across the yawning gap above the Gates of Borrowdale, the wind was up, the temperature down. It looked like some wicked weather was on it's way and, with just T-shirts, shorts and wind-shells for protection we were feeling just a tad under-dressed. Time for a brew. The heavens opened, our empty cafe was suddenly crammed with dripping school kids and Amos declared there's nothing for it but to get on out there. The other two sensibly decided it was time to call it a day. Amos and I had no choice. Our waterproofs were with John. John was snugly ensconced in Buttermere YHA by now.

Out into the deluge and within seconds we were soaked. I shivered. For once I welcomed the prospect of a big hill climb. The heat generated on the long slog up past Ashness Bridge, Surprise View - not surprisingly not a soul was to be seen being 'surprised' - and up past Watendlath (where we were sorely tempted by the teashop.) kept the cold at bay. But nothing prepared us for the tempest that hit us as we crested the rocky outcrops over Grange Fell. An icy blast hurled horizontal shafts of rain in a furore of skin-singeing ferocity. Added to the perils of the precipitous, slick, slippery, rock and rubble run down to Rosthwaite the Cumbrian Mountains had dealt us out a short, sharp bit of shock treatment. A salutary lesson for venturing out under-prepared and over-confident. Down in Rosthwaite we were welcomed into the homely warmth of the hotel, hugged an Aga, sipped soup and steamed gently back into reality. The maitre-de, a Mountain Rescue Team member, reckoned I was teetering on the edge of exposure when we found their fireside. Lesson learned on travelling too light.

As storms go this one was short-lived, if vicious. Bright sun broke through, bathed Borrowdale in honey-coloured light and had us squinting like a pair of owls. Now we needed shades! Of course Amos had his. The haul up Honister - a hard climb by any standards - gave the heat quota a big boost and conquering such a well-known pass without so much as a pause egged on the old ego a notch. But Amos hadn't had his fill of height-gain. He led me up a steep, grassy track where our late afternoon shadows rippled along the rock face alongside. The views would be worth the extra effort, he'd promised. He was right. Out west the vast valley of Buttermere, cut by shadow and shafted light in dramatic perspective steps, reached right to our feet. Below a tiny, ribbon of road snaked its way down from the pass to the valley floor. Time for some roady-type hammertime.

Amos hit top-cog, accelerated off the top of the pass and whipped past a car-load of surprised tourists; still agog when I overtook them seconds later. Rubber hummed, slip-stream roared and I spin out on some chicanes that had the rear tyre stuttering. OK, so once in a while you can wish for some skinny tyres and big gears! Down by Buttermere, with evening shadows spreading a cool blanket across the lake, we sped across the valley and up into the dark embrace of Burness Woods. The day's deluge had still to drain away and the gloopy singletrack that dips and dives through the trees treated us to some rooty, slip 'n slide riding finished off by short and sweet drop down to the valley floor. By the time we pulled into Buttermere YHA the azure skies of a summer's evening had darkened and once more storms threatened. I made sure I watched the weather forecast that night!

BUTTERMERE TO BOOT

Gloom, doom and a drencher of Biblical proportions was promised overnight then delivered on the morrow. John felt fit for a wet foray on the fells - Amos was less enthusiastic but came nevertheless - so we aqua-planed out of the hostel, crossed Buttermere Dubbs on a rough road-turned-river and tried to ignore the ranks of rain that marched up the valley. The rock-strewn singletrack that runs below the Scales is an acid test of technical expertise in the dry. In this wet only 100% commitment, a dogged determination to ride it and a good dose of aggression got us through. But beyond the footbridge riding water-logged peat and grass was beyond even our dogged determination so we picked our way through the mire using the bikes as props.

We filed across the open moors of Mosedale basin for a fun-time of intermittent bog riding, bike carrying and squelching through a soggy morass. The barrier of Mosedale Beck, a ten foot torrent of wild, rushing water, barely slowed Amos - well over 6' and with astride to match - at all. For John and I, both 5' something and short of leg, it was an all-out long jump preceded by a ten yard run-up. A much amused Amos watched our antics and aerobatics. With the river safely behind we scaled the final ridge - a near sheer slope of slippery grass - and walked slap, bang into the storm that, until now, had swept over us. Not just shorts, T- shirt and pertex top now. I was wrapped in the shelter of a storm-proof Polaris jacket and could afford to enjoy the feeling. Especially as we were now able to mount up for the gravity- assisted run down to Ennerdale. A pernicious wind whipped the front wheel about, leading to some unplanned exits off the path, but as the gradient steepened we took on speed and stability. We barrelled down off the wind-swept fells and into the relative calm of Ennerdale. It was an instant transition from the depths of the winter into spring.

Down by Bowness we stopped for a bun and brew and assessed the weather front. It had been hellish up on the hills. Black Sail Pass, 400' higher and a wind tunnel of giant proportions when westerlies blow, would have a screaming typhoon roaring through it. None of us fancied crawling across that col then sliding down to Wasdale so careful counsel ruled caution and we took the road route.

In the warmth of Wasdale's pub we treated ourselves to a bowl of piping hot goulash, grilled our dripping togs by the open hearth and delayed our departure as long as possible. But once we were out in the open, between the cloud-covered shoulders of Scafell and the leaden waters of Wastwater, the spell of space and freedom was on us. Hell, what was a bit of wet 'n wind when it's shared between friends? Track turned to river, singletrack to stream and, in places, cairns to islands isolated in lagoons. They were a nightmare to navigate. Lured on by the disappearing trail you were suddenly floundering about, hitting rocks, hidden holes and the inevitable outcome was a soggy splash-down. We all had a turn. Had a laugh, then egged the victim on for another try. Slime-covered gravel by Burnmoor tarn called for dexterity and power control to avoid a spin-out as befuddled back wheels slued about. If you've ever ridden on a bed of marbles then you'll know what I mean. Weird!

Over Eskdale Moor a unique mix of slick rock and turf turned up the technical quotient that had us weaving in and out in a quest for the best line. Before long the myriad of routes between the boulders concentrated into a rugged, rocky run down the fellside into Boot. The delights and demands of that descent never let up for a moment - we all wiped out somewhere on the way. An exhilarating run if ever there was one. With the YHA full we booked into a fine old farmhouse B&B, down the road at Penny Hill. Tired, wet, elated and with one enormous appetite. With several summits and passes to conquer - after we'd dropped to near sea level on the lower Esk - it was prudent to put the hammer down but the trails down by the river were much too pleasant to blast through. It was already well past lunchtime when we crossed the golf links at Lower Eskholme - a pristine green hemmed in by the ragged heights of the Scafell Pikes that was a bizarre setting to be cycling through - and afternoon was advancing to evening just as we lost our way over to Whitfell.

Well, not quite lost, we knew where we were but the map-makers had misplaced the bridleway path. A neat line of dashes on the map but dashed all on the ground; bar the odd sheep path to be lured along. We trailed to and fro in an effort to find the track, gave up and resorted to compass bearings. When we finally made the grass-covered trail that wound its way up Waberthwaite Fell we looked back to see if we'd managed to miss the map-marked way despite our meandering. Across the flat expanse of heath to the foot of the fell there was no sign of that illusive path. Next time we'd know better and make a bee-line for the fellside!

Forearmed with knowledge that our cartographer had been in creative mode when he drew his dashes we weren't surprised when the trail disappeared again. Happily a handy piece of singletrack took us up to a cairn by Fox Crags and from there it was but a short trek across the col, round the crags of Whitfell and low and behold we found a grass-covered track lurking beneath our tyres. Relief! Undoubtedly we'd been right en-route all the time. Unfortunately it was time that was fast running out. Hit the hammer and high-tail it for Bigert Mire farm.

With all that trudging about the tundra we'd dented the stores somewhat so we re-stocked at Ulpha's post-office and headed for the hills again. Our friendly cartographer had gone crazy with the contours and outlined a load of crags with crinkly lines all over the Dunnerdale Fells. It looked like tempting terrain to ride and the reality proved to be right. Cart tracks climbed contour-by-contour then we spun off into a rugged region of rock and ravine traversed by a tortuous piece of singletrack that roller-coasters its way round to the Lickle valley. The Lickle river really was little! A silver ribbon carving its way down a deep cleft in the fells. We sped along a narrow cut that clung to the side high above the river, risking a slip or two on some slick sections but revelling in both the landscape and the ride.

The valley came to an abrupt end for a serpentine climb-out on grass-covered cart track. A pedestrian push this late in the day. We'd been on the trail for six hours already, climbed nigh on 3000' and fatigue was beginning to make itself felt. We'd yet to make the summit of Walna Scar and I was worried that, tired and weary, we'd make hard work of the descent to Coniston. A descent that's just a brilliant blast when you're in manic mood. By the time we struggled to the top of the pass the sun was setting and there was no time to take ten. Gravity tugged the tyres, smooth track disintegrated, dropped into rock-strewn gullies and it was an eye-blurring, knee-jarring decent that had us shredding the edge of the envelope all the way down. Fatigue forgotten, our spirits soared as we skipped and skidded down to Coniston with a skittish slip or two round the final few bends.

There's nothing like a decent descent to round off the day! But already regrets were in the air. Journey's end was nigh. We'd blasted down the last big downhill and there was just a dozen miles of mellow mud-plugging on the morrow. Then it was over.

FOREST FINALE

Sullen cloud masses swirled around the Old Man's ragged shoulders. It looked like our loop, begun like a lamb, was about to end with some lion-like weather. But by the time we'd hit the road a determined sortie from the sun had dispelled such notions and we quit Coniston with a fine day in prospect.

A loop round the wave-lapped shore of the lake, then we left the road for an ancient by-way that clambers up

Monk Coniston Moor. Often steep, sometimes loose, it was a formidable climb where hanging onto traction was a task in itself. At last the track levelled off, we spun cranks and sped off into the sunlit shelter of Grizedale Forest.

Cruising through flickering light and cool shadows it was a case of kick the cranks, click in top cogs and turn up the speed. A welcome break from wild moors and suicidal singletrack. Loosen up and listen to the slip-stream whistle!

Just as all that tame-trail cruising at speed was beginning to pall we quit forest track for a serpentine pathway slipped in between the trees. Damp and dark our tortuous trail dipped and dived, dealt us the odd drop-off, bog and random lumber to create a radical ride where it's "Don't Think Just Do"! Desperate to stay in front, where it's free from rear tyre mud splatter, each of us fought hard to keep the lead. But way down in the woods, along the leaf-covered track, recent tree-felling had reduced the trail to mega-mire. A morass. Impassively waiting for the arrival of two mud-caked bikers, flying through the forest, vying for poll position.

Singletrack strung us out, John snicked ahead, barrelled in to the bog, ploughed a four foot furrow and stopped. Still astride his steed. A brief hover, legs akimbo - then.... He just stayed there! I slued in beside him. So we left the bikes, bog-bound, and took a break.

Grizedale gave us a short and sweet decent through Devils Gallop then we were out of the woods, humming through bright green pasture-land, along narrow lanes busy with bird-song and sizzling under summer's heat. At first we sauntered. Then, of a sudden, we were fired by the desire to complete the last link in the loop. Lead on by the cool breezes off the lake we coursed round Windermere's winding shore, down the cars queuing for the ferry and fetching up at the waters edge. We sat astride our bikes, watching the ferry approach. Silver waves danced, dashed against the ferry's bow and hurried on to the distant shore. The one which we'd set off from five days before.

BEFORE YOU GO

FITNESS

The Lake District National Park has been the hiker's mountain Mecca for nigh on a century. Now major metropolises are an hour or two's motoring away the peaks and passes are swarming with pedestrians who breeze in for the day, take in a ridge or two, then zip back to the big city. You don't have to be physically very fit to tackle the occasional fell climb and don't believe those who stride the ridges, heads down, grass hissing beneath their heels and who say you do.

But being in shape to take a mountain bike up a mountain is an altogether different thing. You can't pick it up on the trail. And you can't pick it up in the few days before you go. The time to think about getting trim is ten weeks or so before the departure date.

I know it's a long time, puts paid to travelling on a whim and the word 'preparation' rears its ugly head but being fit will make the whole escapade more fun. For everyone. Even MTBers who get out and hit the hills two or three times a month will benefit from some serious working out on their wheels. By the time you get to Bowness (or Penrith) forty miles, fully laden and off-road ought not to be an awesome ordeal.

COMPANIONS

Rides like this are an enriched experience if you're in good company. But travelling companions are notoriously tricky to choose and in the ups and downs betwixt the beginning and the end there will be stresses and strains. Long distance off-roading is not all fun. On precipitous trails it's both difficult and demanding; add fatigue, perhaps a mis-read map and a ferocious wind and you've got a pretty good recipe for a falling out. Always distressing, discord can soon develop into dispute and that could be dangerous, in the wrong place at the wrong time.

Choose companions carefully.

KITTING OUT

HARDWARE

"Weight is wearisome". Whatever you've got you've got to carry it on this trip. And with some seven peaks and passes between 1600' and 2700' you'll appreciate that trimming kit to a necessary minimum makes sense. Providing you don't overdo it and skimp on essentials saving weight is safer too. It conserves energy and makes handling a the bike on some of the more extreme terrain a lot less hairy. Heavy bikes tend to keep going when they get kicked off course!

The Wheels

We're not going to open and have a good probe about in the can of worms that is 'The Best Bike'. To begin with bike choice is a personal choice, fads and fashions change on a whim and providing it's sound any clunker of an MTB will do. Having said that there are some pointers as to what makes a bike well suited to the task and what does not.

You're going to travel some steep and technical trails so use a good quality, reasonably light, proper MTB - 21 or more indexed gears - with alloy wheels, low gearing and a comfortable saddle. We're talking several hundred pounds here but if you're serious about mountain biking it's worth it. Take a look at the mountain biking press for what's what or ask at a good mountain bike shop. Your bike should also be thoroughly serviced and checked out before setting off. A wheel buckle might well bring an early end to your long awaited trip but a collapse could spell disaster so have your wheels trued before you start.

Some bike accessories that should be considered essential are: bottle cages - back-pack drink carriers and rucsacs don't always work together, top and seat tube padding (closed-cell pipe insulation tube is cheap, waterproof and hard-wearing), a brand new set of the best brake blocks you can afford and some branded, good quality treads, with around a 2" carcass of new rubber for cushioning and grip. Consult a good MTB bike shop for what's the latest trend in tyres and avoid cheap 'imitations'.

Other items to consider, especially if long distance off-roading really grabs you, are: Aheadset or a headset lock-ring, Allen-key crank fittings, a bomb-proof set of wheels, heavy duty inner tubes and some sort of suspension, true or otherwise, to fend of fatigue. You may flinch but fitting pedals and clips and not the ubiquitous SPDs offers a firmer footing when it comes to shouldering that frameset and foot slogging. Especially over rocks. Some SPDs also suffer from clogging when it gets really gloopy.

I didn't use a pannier rack on this trip - I felt the extra weight wasn't worth it for the few occasions when a pack could be safely strapped to it. Having said that pannier racks are the next best thing to a mudguard and you might be glad to give your back a rest once in a while. Whatever you do, buy a top quality rack - cheap ones will collapse under the constant stress of trail-shock.

Tools and Spares

Quality doesn't come cheap but good tools are a god-send when you're in a fix so be prepared to pay for them. Most multi-tools will save weight on a tool-roll of separate bits but don't forget to check that your clever widget does all the whatsits on your bike. And your partners'.

The same goes for spares. If you all run the same tyre valves, chains, straddle wires and even brake blocks the stores can be kept to a sensible size. Once you've got all tools and spares together pack them tight and keep them handy - ready for the inevitable trail-side emergency. The Lakeland Loop does take you through England's wildest scenery; even so, there's no need to go over the top with the wilderness thing and go carrying enough spares for a total re-build. Bike shops crop up at regular intervals along the way.

SOFTWARE

Even in summer warmth is the vital ingredient, versatility the name of the game. On the summit of Loadpot Hill it's a lot colder than down by the lake in Howtown. All things being equal. You can be shivering in the icy blast of a savage hailstorm while day-trippers down below are basking in the balmy heat of summer sun. And, with less than half-an-hour of wind screaming in your ears, you'll be down there too: sweating.

Dress sense

Kitting out a mountain biker has proved to be the outdoor clothes designers' biggest challenge yet. It's a strenuous sport, generates loads of heat at peak activity then the loonies stand about mending punctures on a hillside with a wind-chill factor of -10°C and their body temperature drops like the proverbial stone. But designers are rising to the challenge and there's a stack of really good, MTB-specific gear to choose from.

Navigation aids

A good quality compass on a neck cord and weatherproof cycle computer - both of which you must be able to use with ease - and that's the pilot part sorted.

Health and survival gear

Mountain biking can be dangerous; a trivial accident on top of High Street or a major fall on the Furness Fells can quickly bring you down to a survival situation. A matter of life or death. Given the right kit, make the right decisions and you can turn crisis to drama, live to tell the tale and even laugh about it. Later.

A good first aid kit and the knowledge to use it are essential. A basic kit should include anti-sceptic wipes, plasters, cohesive tape for wounds, triangular bandage, salt tablets for cramp, Puritabs and first aid instructions (first aid information, covering some of the common MTB emergencies, is given on separate cards). You might very well be an accomplished first-aider. Whoever comes to your aid might not and they, not to mention you, will appreciate a set of instructions ready to hand.

Survival gear - mini-torch, survival bag and whistle - can all be packed with the first aid kit. Pack it in a heavy-duty, zip-tie polythene bag, label it clearly and know where it is. Not strictly first aid but pretty important to the health department are medicaments for treating minor ailments like saddle soreness (not minor if it happens but Sudacream or E45 cream speeds recovery), athlete's foot, sun burn, lip chaff, muscle strain and pain.

LAKELAND LOOP

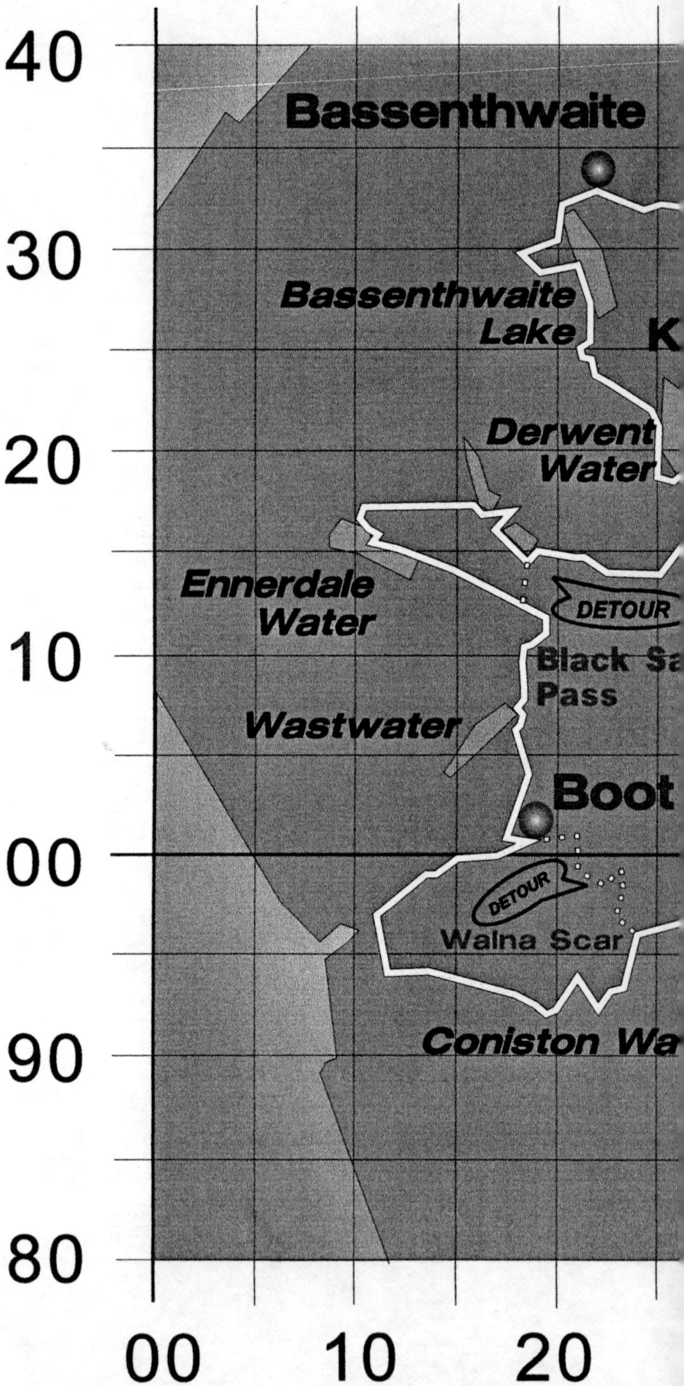

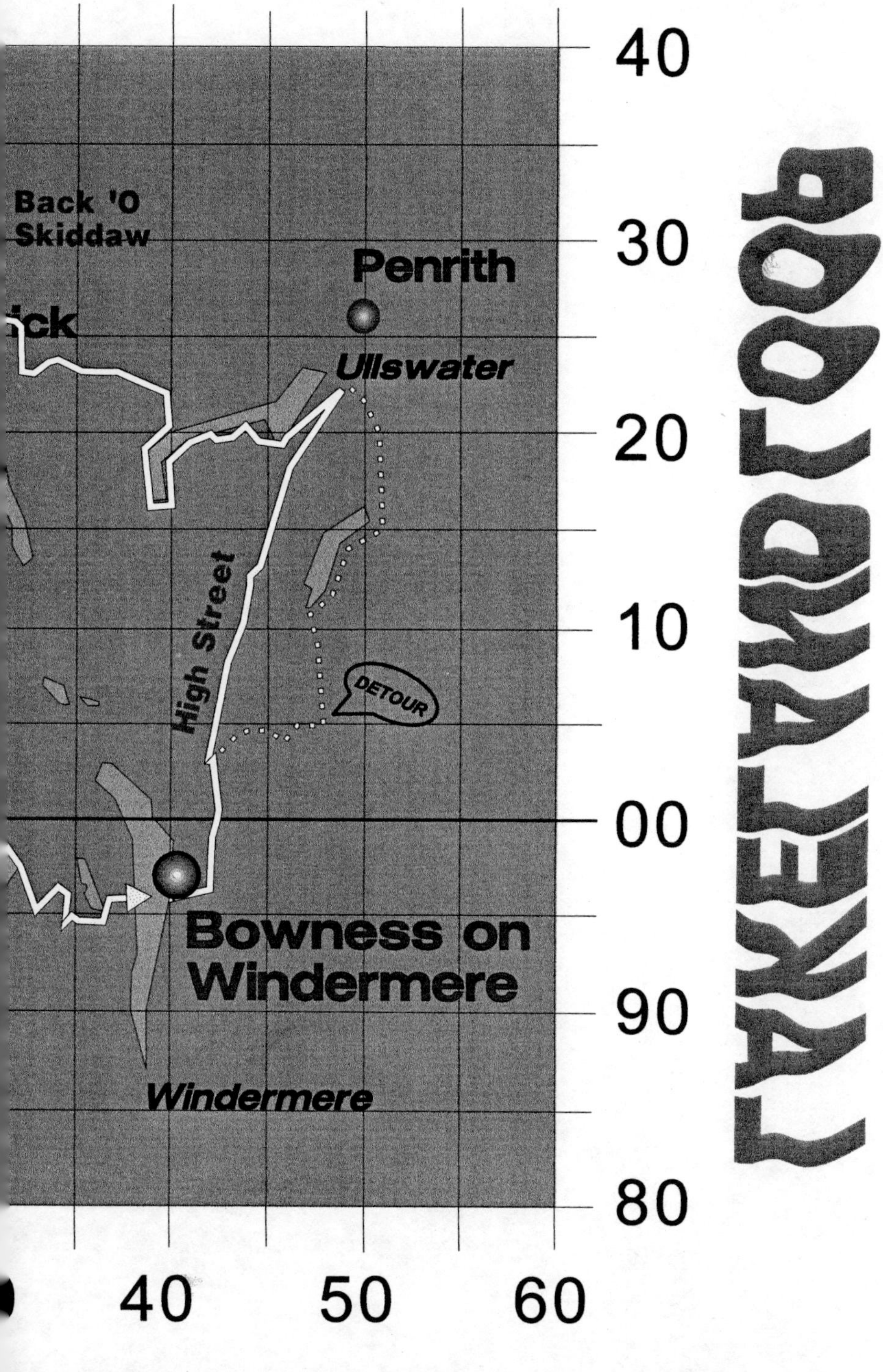
Back 'O
Skiddaw
Penrith
ick
Ullswater
High Street
DETOUR
Bowness on
Windermere
Windermere
40
30
20
10
00
90
80
40
50
60
Lakeland Loop

Other Stuff

Mountain biking's a dirty business so the personal hygiene department needs careful thought. Apart from the usual salves and unguents for bodily application some micro wash-liquid is a good idea to keep those shorts clean and fresh on a day-to-day basis. Remember too that you'll need a small, quick-drying towel.

In the Bag

Fell walkers will be a common sight on parts of the trail - popular walking routes and the ride coincide from time to time - and many of them will be strolling along with pint-sized day-packs to take their kit. Take a leaf out of their book. Travel light and leave it on your back. A small rucsac - about 30l capacity - together with either a bumbag or a small barbag should be fine. Features to look for are a narrow profile, light weight, waist security strap, wide shoulder straps (easily adjusted and locked), low pack height (try it out, packed full, with your helmet on. Bend over forward then look up as though scanning the trail ahead. If the helmet is knocked forwards over your eyes then that's what will happen on the bike) and compression straps. Such features can often be found on climbing and fell-running backpacks but there are a many MTB-specific rucsacs that can be swapped from back to a pannier rack and back with ease.

If you have problems packing all your kit into thirty-odd litres of space then try rolling the clothes into tight cylinders, holding them down and tying them with compression straps (Velcro straps are ideal). Remember to put the least dense gear at the bottom, the heaviest at the top and ensure the back-panel is comfortable against your spine.

LAKELAND LOOP KIT LIST

A handy, pre-'flight' check list is provided but don't regard it as definitive - I habitually carry a pair of mini-Mulgrips, half a toothbrush and a pair of earplugs on these trips. I'll leave you to fathom out why. Lists are an important aid to successful trip planning - a finely honed trip-list is one of the most valuable bits of kit you'll ever use - and making your own will encourage you to evaluate each item on its merits.

Try the list on the next page for starters:

Tool Kit

Pump
Tyre levers
Full set of Allen keys
Small, adjustable wrench
Screwdriver (Cross-head and flat)
Chain-splitter
Spoke key
Penknife

Bike Spares

Inner tube
Puncture repair kit
Brake blocks
Straddle wire
Lube
Rear gear cable
Rear light/batteries
Cable ties
Allen bolts for bottle cages etc.
Gaffer/carpet tape
Couple of spare chain links
Cable lock
Water bottles

Cycle Clothing

Sports socks (3 pairs min.)
Padded shorts (2 pairs min.)
Cool shirt, short-sleeved
Cycle shirt, long-sleeved
Wicking/thermal top
Padded bike mitts
Helmet (Not extreme, elongated, aero-types)
Fleece/mid-layer top
Windproof top
Waterproof top with hood
Tights or windproof over-trousers

MTB Boots

Aprés Trail

Light-weight longs
Underwear
Shorts
Baseball boots/sandals or similar

Personal Kit

Wash kit inc. small, quick-drying towel
Zipped wallet with money
Plastic
SYHA card/B&B contacts
Pencil
Sewing kit (Polyester thread)
Medical kit
Head torch/batteries

Trail Kit

Compass
Computer
1st Aid Kit
Survival kit (Whistle, bag, torch)
Emergency food (Cereal bars etc.)
Rucsac with liner
Seat pack &/or bar/bumbag (to keep emergency kit in)

If you're expecting cold, wet weather then you'll need to add extra clothing, especially thermals (Tights, tops and socks.), full gloves, headband/snood and waterproof socks.
In winter an extra-warm fleece/windproof top, for when you're caught in the open with an emergency repair, lined mitts and lined hood may also be necessary and on the hardware side don't forget front lights. How heavy will this lot weigh? For a summer outing aim for about 12-14lbs for all your personal kit and about 7lbs of shared gear (Including food.). With three up you'll each have about 16lbs of kit on board.

MAPS

1:25000 scale Outdoor Leisure maps 4, 5, 6 and 7

ACCOMMODATION

From the first one of the key considerations is where you are going to sleep. Even how you are going to sleep. Comfort and a good night's rest are keynotes to the success of long distance cycling and only you will know what your absolute needs are. Consider them carefully - you owe it to yourself.

Camping

Camping and self-sufficiency seem to go hand-in-hand with the adventure of mountain biking but - and it's a big but - the penalties are high. Tent, stove, sleeping bag, mat, cooking kit and food plus additional clothes and the out-sized rucsac to put it all in will weigh you down by an extra stone or so and make pass-storming sheer purgatory. Descents are interesting though, if lethal!

Survivors, exhausted by a day beneath their burden, will then have the pleasure of finding a pitch, setting the tent, searching out a stream, fetching the water and washing cold. Then it's cook, eat, clean-up and finally fall into a stupor only to be driven spare at the crack of dawn by a demented bunch of birds doing their dawn chorus thing! Camping's great.

Bed and Breakfast

By way of comparison, at the opposite extreme, we have B&Bs. First and foremost you can dump all that camping kit and ride light. Not day-ride light but nimble enough to loft wheels, bunny hop and skip the rear end round the odd rock. And that's handy. It's fun too!

Add to that an end-of-day cuppa followed by a hot bath, supper in the pub, uninterrupted sleep, a breakfast to build a day's trail blazing on and the pleasure of being the guests of some of the best hosts one could wish for and you've got luxury. But it costs and, in season, prebooking is advisable. That means some sort of timetable.

Youth Hostels

Somewhere between the two alternatives are Youth Hostels. You need only carry the same kit as for B&Bs and they're much cheaper. Most provide a full range of services from shop to showers and if you're not the self-catering type breakfast and evening meal can be a convenient opt-out. Add to that the best YHA idea - the drying room - and you can see hostels are handy.

On the downside mucking in with a bunch of strangers night-on-night isn't always ideal, accommodation is single-sex, in dormitories and sharing a hostel with a bunch of hyper-active juveniles still trying to fight their way free of the education system is not fun! But, all in all, hostels are the best bet and in the Lakes trail-weary bikers are well catered for.

The Lake District is liberally peppered with YHAs and the Lakeland Loop has eleven along it's length - there's a gap up by Bassenthwaite though - and these are listed separately (see the Appendices). Pre-booking is prudent in high-season and be warned; those jolly school parties are a maverick in the accommodation calendar at any time. Many hostels, like B&Bs, have a closed season so the accommodation logistics of a winter circuit need more careful planning.

ON THE RIDE

GETTING THERE

The great thing about the Lakeland Loop is that it begins and ends in the same place, Bowness on Windermere, on the eastern and most accessible side of the National Park. This means you don't have to suffer the pain of getting the train; simply leave the car at the start and ride a round trip.

There is one main road route west from the M6 taking the A590 to the A595 off junction 36, distance 15 miles; from the north it's the A66 to the A592 off junction 40 at Penrith, distance 28 miles.

British railways are not known for being biker-friendly so the key rule is to check, re-check and book everything in advance. Bikes especially! Windermere is served by

Sprinter trains running on a branch line. A 'worse case scenario' so far as bike carrying is concerned - though the rolling stock used should take three or four bikes - and you may well be better off starting from Penrith. It's on the mainline and just half a dozen miles north of the Loop where it passes close to Pooley Bridge.

FELL-RIDING

Ride safe. Ride light. Still labelled as the new boys on the block mountain bikers run the gauntlet of being alienated by other countryside users. The sport has mushroomed and our wilderness areas have witnessed a wheeled invasion - ramblers see us as rivals, environmentalists call us erosionists and farmers fear speeding bikes will frighten stock and uncaring cyclists will flatten crops.

The fact that it's a re-run of early rambler versus landowner conflicts makes no difference. Neither does the fact that the hoary chestnuts of "tyres tear up trails " and "bikers are the beasts of the bridleways" are perceived, not proven, concerns of some of our countryside companions. But we're here to stay and entrenched attitudes are already changing and this will come about more quickly if we ride responsibly.

Rights of Way

Although we've taken every care to try and ensure that the Lakeland Loop route will keep your cycling within the law, at the very least the status of some sections is likely to change.

Plus, of course, you may get lost so it is as well to be sure of your rights of way.

Off-road cycling is permitted on bridleways, roads used as public paths (RUPPs), by-ways open to all traffic (BOATs), unclassified county roads (greenways) and designated cycle paths. Some of the Forestry Commission and North West Water Authority roads are open to us with the landowner's consent and this permissive access may be revoked at any time. Cycling is not permitted on footpaths, open land or on pavements. Do not rely on signposts as reliable indicators of a route's status - bridleway (blue) and footpath (yellow). If in doubt dismount. And remember, all land is owned by someone - even the remote moorland areas on this route - and you must take care not to trespass. If a landowner asks that you leave it is in your best interests, no matter what the right and wrong of it may be, to acquiesce.

Of course you may be bowling along a bridleway when up pops a barbed wire fence and the way is barred. It's a tricky situation because your rights are wrapped in a woolly bit of rhetoric which says you can remove the obstacle sufficiently to get past if it is reasonably possible or make a short detour to get round it. The landowner can demand recompense if you cause any damage so clambering over it - often the instinctive reaction - is not a clever thing to do. This doesn't happen often but Rights of Way across farmland do get blocked, ploughed up, are over-planted or are stocked with dangerous animals. Farmers are supposed to provide signed, alternative routes but if you're in doubt don't traipse across regardless. Check with the owner and if you're still forced off the Right of Way report it to the local authority - addresses are given in the Appendices - who will take up the matter on your behalf.

Codes of Conduct

In following the Lakeland Loop off-road route you will be treading in the tyre tracks of others. If they've careered along, forged furrows across fields, stampeded livestock, left gates gaping and created a trail of havoc and mayhem then you're not going to get a warm reception from the countryside community. Nor is anybody else who follows along unless you follow the Country and Off-road Codes.

Enjoy the countryside and respect its life and work
Guard against all risk of fire
Fasten all gates
Keep dogs under control
Keep to Public Rights of Way across farmland
Use gates and stiles to cross boundaries
Leave livestock, crops and machinery alone
Take your litter home
Do not contaminate water

Protect wild flora and fauna
Take special care on country roads
Make no unnecessary noise
Cycle only on permitted Rights of Way
Give way to horse riders and walkers
Do not ride so that you are a danger to others
Do not race
Keep erosion to a minimum and do not skid
Be courteous and considerate to others
Be self-sufficient and make sure your bike is safe to ride
Wear a helmet
Follow a route marked on a map
Follow the Country Code

They're not really a set of rules so much as guidances that any responsible, thoughtful member of the mountain biking community would adopt without a second's thought.

Ride safety

Three's company, not two, and four's fine outdoors in the wilds. In the event of one getting badly injured someone can go for help and someone can stay with the casualty. But ideally two should go for help, not one, which is why four is better. More and mountain bikers in a bunch can be an intimidating party on a narrow path.

Abilities, strength and stamina in any group will vary. Keep within the capacity of everyone, watch your pace and make sure everyone keeps within sight and sound of each other. But don't bunch up, especially on downhills, or there'll be some rear-end wipe-outs. And they can be real nasty! It's always a good idea to wait for stragglers at the top of climbs, at the bottom of tricky descents and at gates. It's in the nature of a strung out group to separate even further at such points so make sure that the young, eager pup out in front is aware of it.

One of the first signs of fatigue is when your normally ebullient companion rides quiet and persistently lags behind. Don't push it. Rest, drink, eat and keep warm - exposure may be just around the corner.

Weather

Out in the wilds weather will make or break a day. In northern England it's notoriously variable and up in the fells it's all in a day's weather to experience sun, sleet, rain, wind, warmth, cold and calm. Maybe the Cumbrian Mountains are small on the global scale but they don't act like it. It's easy be lulled into a false sense of security, set out ill-informed and unprepared and end up the subject of a fell rescue operation. I know. I did exactly that - set off without listening to the forecast - and had a close call with exposure as a result! Get the most recent weather forecast - telephone numbers are given in the Appendices - and make a habit of catching the latest TV weather forecasts. They give a useful overview of what's coming.

Three factors that strangers to the fells often fail to take into account are altitude, wind and winter. As you climb temperature falls. Roughly speaking temperature falls 1C° for every 100m gain in height (3C° per 1000') on a clear day, half that fall on a cloudy one. Wind-chill increases with wind strength. In a gentle to moderate breeze (force 3, about 10mph) wind- chill is about -5C°, about -10C° in a fresh, gusty breeze (force 5, about 20mph) and -15C° in a really strong wind (force 7, about 30mph). For example on a clear, calm day the temperature on Black Sail Pass will be about 5C° colder than down in the garden of Ennerdale YHA. Add in the cooling effect of the inevitable wind, say a brisk breeze, and up on the Pass temperatures will dip a chilling 12C° or so! Even in summer temperature frequently falls to 5°C, in mid-winter we're talking down another 10-14C°. That's 9° below zero! Makes you think, doesn't it?

It would be foolish to venture out onto the Cumbrian Mountains if strong winds are forecast knowing that they'll be more ferocious on the higher fells. Take a day's furlough and live to bike another day. And be prepared to take an unplanned detour around passes and peaks if the wind builds during the day.

Forecasts give temperatures but it's as well to bear in mind, when planning a departure date, that winter temperatures will be 10-15C° colder than summer ones. Nippy!

LOSING YOUR WAY

Navigation can be tricky. Keeping on course depends on you, and preferably your companions as well, knowing your position at ALL times. Danger zones are forests, open moor and in poor visibility so take care to read the terrain correctly in these situations and make no assumptions about this or that trail being a 'main' route. One way of coping with poor visibility is to follow a compass bearing to the most distant visible marker (not a sheep because it might walk off!), cycle to it, take another bearing on the next marker, cycle and so on.

With very few exceptions - over Waberthwaite Fell is one and into Swindale via Mosedale is about the only other - you'll be riding on obvious tracks and paths so you are more likely to feel lost than really be lost. But, despite our best endeavours to keep you on track, there's always a chance you might wander from the route. Nobody intends to get lost and it comes as a shock.

Don't panic. Stop. Make sure everybody's with you and then try to work out where you went wrong. Not too far back you'll have been sure of your position. Find it on the map. Naturally you'll have been using your cycle computer to keep a log of point-to-point distances and it's a simple matter of reading the distance off, calculating direction and that'll give you an approximate position.

Forgotten to zero the trip distance at the last known point? Then estimate how long ago you were there and in which direction you have travelled during the elapsed time. Allowing for ground conditions, calculate how far you've cycled. Now check your surroundings and see if local landmarks coincide with your findings. If you're still unsure and visibility is poor then stay put until conditions improve.

In an ideal world three distinct landmarks should be recognised for you to be absolutely certain of your locality though, given two, you can still take compass bearings to position yourself. It goes without saying that correct use of the compass and trusting it, not your instincts, is vital.

ACCIDENT PROCEDURE

It's vital too that at least one of the party is a qualified first-aider. Ideally all of you should know the fundamentals of first aid. The British Red Cross, St John's Ambulance and St Andrew's Ambulance Societies all run courses so, if you haven't done already, book into one. One day, somebody will thank you for it.

It can't be over-emphasised that carrying a proper first aid kit with instructions and being a competent first aider is an essential part of accident procedure. But first aid instructions don't always cover the common illness and injuries associated with wild country mountain biking. These are given in the Appendices.

BIKE CARE

Before Riding

A routine check-up should include brake blocks, tyres, wheels and gears. It's a good idea to keep an eye on the chain, headset, stem, cranks and seat post. Don't forget to lube the chain daily.

After Riding

Treat your bike kindly and it'll be a reliable friend. At the end of a day hammering trails the last thing you want to do is bike maintenance but at the very least you should wash off the worst cack with water then give cables, mechs and chain a dose of water-displacer. Do this right after a ride when the mud slips off easily then check it over whilst you remember all those little mechanicals that have been niggling you during the ride.

HOW TO USE THE ROUTE CARDS

Firstly you need to highlight the route on your maps by 'following' the route directions in conjunction with the master map in the centre of this booklet. Occasional six-figure grid references (GR) are given to ensure you mark the correct route (help on calculating a GR is included with the route cards). Paragraph numbers are used to annotate maps so that you can quickly match a particular instruction with a position on the map. To protect the cards on the trail carry it in an 'A5' size clear plastic, zipped document case. Always carry a map ready folded to show the terrain you are crossing.

ROUTE ABBREVIATIONS AND INSTRUCTIONS

Instructions are brief and to the point and follow a uniform format that are designed to give most help whilst on the trail.

The following abbreviations are used:

SO	straight on/over
L	left
R	right
LH	left-hand
RH	right-hand

Route instructions are split into small, point-to-point sections with your accumulated trip distance given at the beginning of each paragraph. You may find some divergence between your computer display and these distances - this is normal.

Primary compass bearings and additional information are often given (in brackets) for further clarification.

DAILY ROUTE TASTERS

DAY 1

BOWNESS-ON-WINDERMERE TO PATTERDALE

30 miles (25 miles off-road)

Summits: High Street - 2700ft; High Raise - 2650ft; Loadpot Hill - 2100ft.

Passes: Applethwaite Common - 950ft.

Lake Windermere, England's largest lake, is quickly left behind as tarmac takes you up 550' to Cleabarrow where you get your first taste of track on this 150 mile loop of the Lakeland Mountains. It's a tame intro but then that's just as well. Day one is a big one. The big climb is the 1400' carry to crest High Street - site of a local fayre that featured hair-raising horse races round the cliff-tops - but then there's some big, big views when you get there. After that the rest's a doddle. Bar some minor mounts -Rampsgill Head, High Raise, Wether Hill and Loadpot - you're in for a rare treat; the long, long descent to Ullswater where waits some extraordinarily tasty singletrack with views to match.

The first rocky run down to Riggindale is along an edge; remember that the extra weight will make the bike a bit unwieldy so don't go wild and get airborne. And please don't forget to walk through farmyards when asked to - the dales are a workplace too. If it's blowing a hooly then take the low route via Kentmere and Gatesgarth Pass.

DAY 2

PATTERDALE TO BASSENTHWAITE

23 miles (13 miles off-road)

Summits: High Row - 1340ft; Old Coach Road - 1450ft.
Passes: Whitewater Dash - 1600ft.

After yesterday you'll need a bit of saunter when all the climbing can be done in the saddle. There's some easy, lakeside tarmac to stretch quivering quadriceps but it's busy bit of road in season and, remember, most biking accidents happen on road. Take care. The climb to High Row's a steady, minor-cog slog - you pass the access to Aira Force falls on the way if you want a breather - but the Old Coach Road is a good blast alongside the blasted heath of Threlkeld Common. It all finales on a fine, downhill dash with some bends and bumps to give your heartbeat a boost.

Back to tarmac with the tricky crossing of the A66 to Threlkeld where the pub's a perfect spot for lunch. Don't over-do the eating though; the climb to the Blencathra Centre - where the National Park's regional offices are located - is no picnic. Then some more up to Skiddaw House YHA - one of the most remote buildings in England.

Beyond are two fast-track descents of demonic dimensions! But only if they're pedestrian-free. Take on speed with caution - it's a touch dicey round the Dash Falls.

DAY 3

BASSENTHWAITE TO BUTTERMERE

30 miles (9 miles off-road)

Summits: Thornthwaite Forest - 820ft.

Passes: Grange Fell - 1100ft; Honister Pass - 1200ft.

OK, so there's a good deal of road riding today but its got the highest scenic quotient of The Loop and sandwiches some truly sweet off-roading including a radical, rut and rubble ride into Rosthwaite. Watch out for those dastardly drainage ditches!

After that one you'll need a road rest so you can enjoy the excursion through beautiful Borrowdale - Britain's wettest place -right in the heart of the Lake's most spectacular scenery. And, talking of sandwiches, there's tea-stops galore along the way including Grange, High Lodore, Watendlath and Rosthwaite.

Honister is a bit of a haul - the first half-mile is the hardest -but the hell-for- leather blast to Buttermere is a must for macadam addicts. When the slip-stream stops screaming it's back to track for a delightful, if dirty, wind-down to Buttermere.

DAY 4

BUTTERMERE TO ESKDALE

24 miles (20 miles off-road)

Passes: Whiteoak Moss (Floutern Tarn) - 1300ft; Black Sail Pass - 1800ft; Burnmoor - 990ft.

A bit short on miles but long on height gain. Testing singletrack kicks off the day before a big climb over bleak fells with a bog-trot or two. Vague pathways can be disheartening - just make sure you head west, up-valley and pass to the north of Floutern Tarn. Once you're beyond it it's some well-deserved downhilling into Ennerdale. A remote dale dominated by the peak of Pillar - 2925ft - said to be the only Cumbrian mountain that has to be climbed. Beyond the delightful and remote Black Sail YHA is the pass. The Loop's second official carry. 850ft to the col then some more down the far side before the loose path firms up for the zigzag drop into Wasdale Head. Tricky!

After some R 'n R in the pub take stock of river heights. If they're full use the Bad Weather Route even it's sunny at the time. The rocky climb up to the moors above Burnmoor Tarn is really a short carry round the shoulders of Scafell Pike -England's highest summit at 3210ft. Once you're up there follow the cairn-marked bridleway round the tarn for a one of the best bits of downhilling in the Lakes to Boot.

DAY 5

ESKDALE TO CONISTON

26 miles (22 miles off-road)

Summits: Whitfell - 1600ft; The Grounds - 900ft.

Passes: Brown Pike (Walna Scar Road) - 2000ft.

Today's going to take longer than you think. First you're going to drop to sea-level as near as makes no odds, then climb Whitfell, drop right back down again and then climb over the highest pass on the route - Walna Scar. It's also slow going on the non-existent trails over Waberthwaite Fell. So be prepared! But don't despair there's some fine riding to be had. The cart-tracks of Eskdale are a delight, the Dunnerdale Fells feature sections of really special singletrack and the boulder-hopping race down to Coniston is one extreme exit from the hills. Heart-stopping stuff! Ulpha PO, about half-way, is your only opportunity to take on extra supplies.

DAY 6

CONISTON TO BOWNESS-ON-WINDERMERE

11 miles (6 miles off-road)

Summits: Grizedale Forest - 830ft.

With the end in sight it's wind-down time. If you've got all day then get into Grizedale and have some fun in the forest - there's absolutely loads of track and trails to explore. Grizedale Visitor Centre has details and maps. For dedicated Loopers the last half-dozen miles of off-road is a good mix of fast forest fire-road and sinuous, rooty singletrack with some short 'n sweet descents.

Remember the forest is an industrial environment and you may meet trucks, vans and other bikers on any bend. It's a short, chicaned road ride to the shores of Windermere and the waiting ferry. They run half-hourly, you can use either the foot or vehicle boats and on the 15 minute crossing you can reflect on the last six days of superlative riding.

Seems to have shot by!

APPENDICES

MAPS

1:25000 scale Outdoor Leisure maps 4, 5, 6 and 7

The following pages are a directory of useful contacts for the Lakeland Loop off-road cyclist including YHAs, bike shops, National Park, National Trust, Forest Enterprise, Local Authority and Association offices.

WEATHER NEWS

Lake District in detail Tel: 01768 775757 (normal rates)
Cumbria Weatherline Tel: 0891 500 419
Mountaincall Tel: 0891 500 483

YOUTH HOSTELS ASSOCIATION

Trevelyan House, 8 St Stephen's Hill, St Albans, Herts AL1 2DY Tel: 01727 855215

YHA Northern England Region for Camping Barn information

Tel: 01629 824571

YOUTH HOSTELS (EN-ROUTE)

High Cross, Windermere	Tel: 015394 43543
Patterdale	Tel: 017684 82394
Greenside, Helvellyn	Tel: 017684 82269
Skiddaw House	Tel: 016974 78325 (Carrock Fell YHA)
Derwent Water	Tel: 017687 77246
Longthwaite, Borrowdale	Tel: 017687 77257
Honister Hause	Tel: 017687 77267
Buttermere	Tel: 017687 70245
Ennerdale	Tel: 01946 861237
Black Sail Hut, Ennerdale	(no telephone)
Eskdale	Tel: 019467 23219
Coniston	Tel: 015394 41323
Hawkshead	Tel: 015394 36293

BIKE SHOPS

Keswick

Keswick Mountain Bike Centre, Dalestone Court. Tel: 017687 75202

Lakeland Pedlar, Bell Close. Tel: 017687 75752

Penrith

Arragons' Cycle Centre, 2 Brunswick Road. Tel: 01768 890344

Grizedale

Wheelbase MTB Hire Centre, Grizedale Forest Park Centre. Tel: 01229 860369

Windermere

Lakeland Leisure, Station Precinct. Tel: 015394 44786

Staveley (nr Windermere)

Wheelbase, Staveley Mill Yard, Staveley. Tel: 01539 821443

Ambleside

Bike Treks, 2 Millans Park. Tel: 015394 31245

Gyhllside Cycles, The Slack. Tel: 015394 33592

BRITISH RAIL BOOKING INFORMATION

National Tel: 0345 484950

TOURIST INFORMATION CENTRES

Windermere	Tel: 015394 46499
Ambleside	Tel: 015394 32582
Patterdale	Tel: 017684 82414
Keswick	Tel: 017687 72645
Whitehaven	Tel: 019466 95678
Ravenglass	Tel: 012297 17278

NATIONAL PARK OFFICES

Lake District Nat Pk, Brockhole, Windermere, Cumbria LA23 1LJ. Tel: 019662 6601

FOREST ENTERPRISE OFFICES

Lakes Forest District, Grizedale, Hawkshead, Ambleside, Cumbria LA22 0QJ. Tel: 01229 860373

NATIONAL TRUST

Cumbria - The Hollens, Grasmere, Ambleside LA22 9QZ. Tel: 015394 35599

COUNTY COUNCIL (RIGHTS OF WAY)

Highways and Transportation, County Offices, Kendal, Cumbria LA9 4RG. Telephone 01539 814346.

GRID REFERENCE HELP

OS maps describe how to obtain a grid reference (GR) in the margin of their maps. MBRUK route cards use six-figure grid references - two sets of three numbers to give an 'easting' and a 'northing'. The first two numbers of each set of three refer to the grid lines on the 1:50000 Landranger and 1:25000 Outdoor Leisure, Explorer and Pathfinder maps (printed large in the example below), the last number in each set of three refers to an imaginary 1/10th line (printed small in the example below) which you use in the same way as the cross-hairs in a gun-sight to 'target' the location.

The 'easting' set of numbers is always given before the 'northing' set. Incidentally most over-the-counter GPS units are only accurate enough for 6 figure GRs.

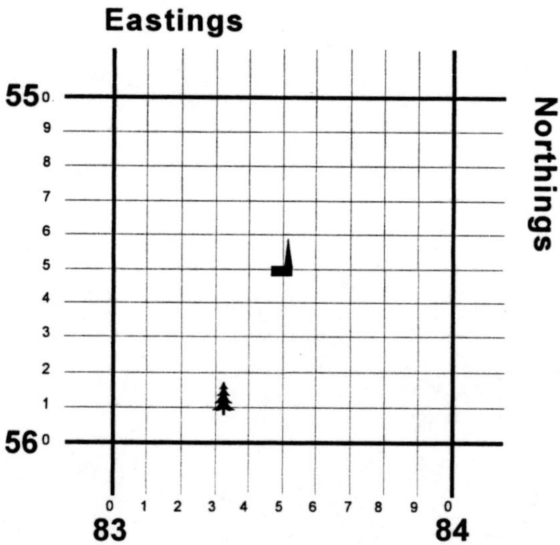

6 figure grid reference is 835 565

6 figure grid reference is 833 561

OTHER MBRUK ROUTE GUIDES

The COAST-TO-COAST Mountain Bike Ride	*The classic St Bees to Robin Hood's Bay route. Our Holy Grail trail.*
The SARN HELEN TRAIL Mountain Bike Ride	*Follow an ancient Roman road through the heart of Wales*
The SCOTLAND TRAIL Mountain Bike Ride	*This Highland C-t-C is thought by many to be Britain's best off-road tour*
The HIGH PEAK TRAIL Mountain Bike Ride	*Figure of '8' tour through Dark & White Peaks with options to split it into two*
The WESTCOUNTRY WAY Mountain Bike Ride	*Cross Dartmoor, Exmoor & the Quantock Hills to enjoy a great mix of trails*
The WESSEX WAY Mountain Bike Ride	*Ideal tyro's tour across the Mendips, Salisbury Plain and South Downs*

CHECK OUT OUR WEBSITE ON:

http://www.mbruk.co.uk